MYSTERIES IN HISTORY

How Did Rome Rise and Fall?

Solving the Mysteries of the Past

Anita Croy

Cavendish
Square
New York

Published in 2018 by Cavendish Square Publishing, LLC
243 5th Avenue, Suite 136 New York, NY 10016

Website: cavendishsq.com

© 2018 Brown Bear Books Ltd

Library of Congress Cataloging-in-Publication Data

Cataloging-in-Publication Data

Names: Croy, Anita.
Title: How did Rome rise and fall? / Anita Croy.
Description: New York : Cavendish Square, 2018. | Series: Mysteries in history: solving the mysteries of the past | Includes index.
Identifiers: ISBN 9781502628060 (library bound) | ISBN 9781502628077 (ebook)
Subjects: LCSH: Archaeology and history--Italy--Rome--Juvenile literature. | Excavations (Archaeology)--Italy--Rome--Juvenile literature. | Rome (Italy)--Antiquities--Juvenile literature. | Rome--History--Juvenile literature. | Rome--Social life and customs--Juvenile literature.
Classification: LCC DG65.C35 2018 | DDC 937--dc23

For Brown Bear Books Ltd:
Editorial Director: Lindsey Lowe
Managing Editor: Tim Cooke
Children's Publisher: Anne O'Daly
Design Manager: Keith Davis
Designer: Lynne Lennon
Picture Manager: Sophie Mortimer

Contents

Who Built the City?

The ancient Romans were not the first people to build a city on the banks of the Tiber River in Central Italy, but their city became one of the greatest cities in history.

When Rome was founded in the 700s BCE, there were already cities in central Italy. Rome was no different from its neighbors. Yet, within 500 years, Rome ruled most of the Mediterranean Sea. It would become the world's largest city.

The Tiber River became a highway for goods arriving in Rome by boat.

The Roman **empire** was the largest empire that had ever existed at the time. How the small farming settlement on the banks of the Tiber rose to become a world power is one of the great stories of history.

IN CONTEXT

The Italian Peninsula
Rome was built on a hilly site on the Tiber River in west-central Italy. As the city grew, it took over rich farmlands in the heart of the Italian **peninsula**. Meanwhile, the peninsula was protected from invasion by the Mediterranean Sea and by the Alps Mountains in northern Italy.

Alps

•Rome

Mediterranean Sea

The Etruscans built the first town of Rome. They buried their dead in underground tombs.

The Etruscans

The Etruscans lived in central Italy between 750 and 250 BCE, when they came under the control of the Romans. They had their own king, language, and religion. They developed trade networks in the eastern Mediterranean region. The Romans took over many aspects of Etruscan culture, such as building methods, **terracotta** pottery, and wall painting.

The ancestors of the Romans were the Latins and Sabines. These farmers settled on the hilly site in the 1100s BCE. For many years, they fought with their neighbors, the Etruscans.

The Republic

In 753 BCE, the Etruscans defeated the Latins and Sabines. They took over the land and built the first town on the site of Rome. The Latins and Sabines continued to fight against the Etruscan king in Rome.

The Etruscans built walled towns such as Volterra, in Tuscany, Italy.

↑ The Roman Senate was eager to spread Rome's power as widely as possible.

The Etruscans were finally defeated in 509 BCE and the Latins and Sabines took back their territory. They then began to develop a system of government known as a **republic**. Instead of the city being ruled by a king, the citizens—who were now called Romans—made the decisions. There was a Senate made up of members of old landowning families, and an Assembly, which was made up of ordinary people. Senators had a lot of power. They were eager to bring more territory under Rome's control.

Expansion

Rome soon became the most important state in Italy. The power of the city grew as a result of military **strategy** and the ambitions of the members of the Senate. Roman armies defeated Rome's neighbors in a series of wars. The Romans made deals with their defeated neighbors.

In return for protecting people in times of war, Roman soldiers stayed in the cities they had conquered. This military **occupation** soon gave Rome control of most of central and southern Italy. Rome allowed the peoples it conquered to buy the right to govern themselves in exchange for paying taxes to Rome. This money helped Rome to grow rich.

A Trading Network

Tradespeople followed Rome's soldiers into defeated territory. There was soon a busy and profitable trading network across Rome's growing empire.

In Roman mythology, Rome was founded by twin brothers named Romulus and Remus. They were said to have been fed by a female wolf.

↑ These walls were once part of buildings in ancient Rome.

As Roman territory spread beyond the Italian peninsula, Rome came to dominate the Mediterranean Sea. Romans called the Mediterranean *Mare Nostrum*, Latin for "Our Sea."

For nearly 500 years after the founding of the Republic in 509 BCE, the Romans expanded their territory through warfare. Roman armies conquered North Africa to the south and Syria to the east. They also conquered much of Europe, including lands that are now Greece, France, and Spain.

SCIENCE SOLVES IT

Dating the City

Using laser scanners and high-definition photography, experts have shown that Rome is older than was traditionally believed. Tests on a wall in central in Rome show that it dates back to 900 BCE. The date comes from **radiocarbon dating** of fragments of ceramics, grain, and rock in the walls. Tests suggest that the city may have been founded 200 years earlier than the Romans themselves had believed.

Rome's First Dictator

Julius Caesar (100–44 BCE) is one of the most famous of all Roman leaders. William Shakespeare wrote the play *Julius Caesar* about him. Caesar expanded Roman territory by conquering France. He defeated the Egyptians and fell in love with Egypt's queen, Cleopatra. Caesar was **assassinated** on March 15, a date known as the Ides of March, in 44 BCE. The plot against him was led by two senators, Cassius and Brutus, who thought Caesar had taken too much power for himself.

This painting from 1865 shows the murder of Julius Caesar by members of the Roman Senate in 44 BCE.

The Romans organized these conquered lands as provinces. Each province had its own governor who was chosen by the Senate in Rome. Roman settlers introduced their own customs and culture to the provinces, although they also absorbed local influences. In order to keep soldiers loyal to Rome they were given land in the territory they conquered.

The Empire Emerges

Members of the Senate fought over control of Rome's expanding territory. The Senate split into different groups, each of which wanted power. The military rulers seized their chance to take power from the Senate. In 49 BCE, Julius Caesar seized power. Other military **dictators** followed. The early dictators had severe limits placed on their power by the citizens. But later dictators ignored the Senate and the Assembly and ruled Rome as they wanted.

In 27 BCE, one of Caesar's descendants declared himself emperor. He called himself Augustus. He was the founder of the Roman Empire and ruled until his death in 14 CE. The Roman Empire lasted from 27 BCE until 476 CE. For more than 500 years between 100 BCE and 400 CE, Rome was the largest city in the world.

Augustus declared himself the first emperor of Rome in 27 BCE.

What Made Rome Eternal?

Today, Rome is known as the eternal city. Its ancient buildings are reminders of the power the Roman empire once held across the world.

There has been a settlement on the banks of the Tiber River for over 1,000 years. The modern city of Rome is built on top of or alongside traces from the ancient city. Every year, **archaeologists** find exciting new discoveries that tell experts a little more about how the Romans lived.

The ruins of the ancient Forum, or meeting place, still stand in the middle of the modern city.

↑ The Colosseum was a huge arena used for public entertainment.

The Roman City

Over the last 200 years, archaeologists have pieced together a picture of what life was like in ancient Rome. They have made discoveries that helped them understand how and why the city rose to become so important and powerful before its eventual decline and fall.

The Forum was at the heart of ancient Rome. It was the **ceremonial** center of the city. It was a large open area used for business, government, worship, and shopping. The buildings around the Forum were once some of the most important in Rome. They were temples, government offices, and businesses. Today's ruins give some idea of how large the buildings might have been.

The open space of the Forum was surrounded by temples and public buildings.

IN CONTEXT

The Roman Forum

The Forum was the spiritual and political heart of ancient Rome. The most important temples stood there. Even when it was surrounded by buildings, the space continued to be the most important meeting place for Romans and their rulers. Wealthy or powerful Romans erected monuments and statues in the Forum to remind the Roman people of their status.

A building called the Colosseum stood near the Forum. It was a huge **amphitheater** built in 80 CE to provide ordinary Romans with an entertainment arena. Roman emperors knew that it was in their interests to keep their citizens happy, so they staged many public events for them. The Colosseum could seat up to 50,000 people.

Citizens watched fights between **gladiators** or reenactments of famous battles. Smaller versions of the Colosseum were built throughout the Roman Empire to provide similar entertainment.

Engineering Skills

One of the most remarkable Roman buildings still standing is the Pantheon. It is nearly 2,000 years old.

The domed ceiling of the Pantheon was a feat of engineering.

This raised **aqueduct** carried water into the heart of Rome.

The Pantheon was a temple. The Romans worshiped many gods. The Pantheon is unique because it is the only temple that honored all the gods together.

The Pantheon is evidence of the engineering skill that helped the Romans build their empire. Its original domed roof still stands. Ancient Roman engineers constructed the dome from a type of **concrete** that was relatively light but also very strong. They designed the dome as one span supported by a series of arches. They hollowed out panels inside the roof to make the weight of the dome lighter. The whole roof also becomes thinner toward the top. At the top, the concrete is just 4 inches (10 cm) thick.

Expert Engineering

In the first two centuries CE, the emperors tried to make the city as modern as they could. They wanted to make sure that the 2 million people living in the city were content. This helped to prevent the citizens rioting against the emperors.

The emperors ordered fresh water be brought to Rome. Engineers designed a network of pipes and aqueducts to carry water into the city from springs in the countryside. The water was carried to fountains and bathhouses. Only the richest could afford their own bathroom, so the emperors built public bathhouses with hot and cold water. Bathing was an important pastime. People met their friends at the baths.

Roman engineers also built roads, walls, and even shopping malls across the empire. The roads followed straight lines. They helped the Roman army move around as quickly as possible.

These underground ruins in Rome likely belonged to a complex of stores, similar to a shopping mall.

17

The emperor Augustus built his palace on the Palatine Hill in Rome.

Exciting Discoveries

After he became the first emperor of Rome in 27 BCE, Augustus, built a palace on the Palatine Hill, one of Rome's Seven Hills. In 2007, archaeologists were **excavating** the ruined palace when they came across an unexpected find. As they drilled into the ground beneath the palace to see if it was stable, the drill broke through into a mysterious empty space.

The experts pushed a camera on a long probe through the hole. The pictures revealed a round cave. Its walls were lined in **mosaics**, marble, and seashells. The experts believed they had found a sacred cave used for religious rituals. Some people thought the cave might be linked to the legend of Romulus and Remus and the founding of Rome.

ANCIENT SECRETS

A Sacred Cave

The cave on the Palatine Hill may be a sacred cave that was recorded by ancient Roman writers. This was the Lupercal. *Lupa* means "she-wolf" in Latin, and the ancient Romans linked the cave to the legend of the founding of Rome. A female wolf found twin babies, Romulus and Remus, floating on the Tiber River. She saved them and fed them in her cave on the Palatine Hill. Some people think the cave is the birthplace of Rome.

← The walls of the cave on the Palatine Hill are covered with mosaics made from small pieces of colored stone.

Where Did the Romans Live?

In 212 CE, the Emperor Caracalla granted full Roman citizenship to any free man who lived in the Roman Empire.

Millions of people claimed citizenship of Rome. Some lived thousands of miles from the city. At the height of its power, the Roman Empire stretched from Syria in the east to Spain in the west and south to North Africa and Egypt. It also spread north to England's border with Scotland. Roman citizens could live anywhere within this huge territory.

This carving shows Roman soldiers in the 100s CE.

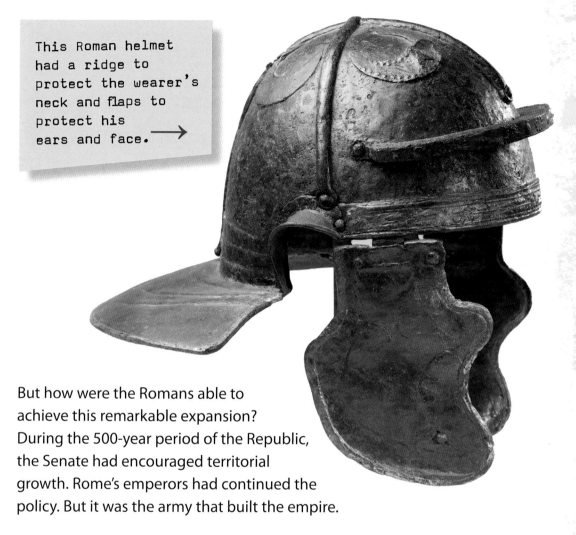

This Roman helmet had a ridge to protect the wearer's neck and flaps to protect his ears and face. →

But how were the Romans able to achieve this remarkable expansion? During the 500-year period of the Republic, the Senate had encouraged territorial growth. Rome's emperors had continued the policy. But it was the army that built the empire.

The Roman Army

Roman soldiers were called legionaries. They underwent a strict training program and were expected to march as far as 20 miles (32 km) a day. They learned how to fight the enemy at close range, and were almost unbeatable in battle. Legionaries were organized into groups of 80 to 100 men. The groups were called centuries. Each century was led by a skilled soldier called a centurion. There were 59 centuries in a legion and the army had 30 legions.

Legions were often recruited from different conquered peoples. These legions were sent anywhere in the empire where they might be needed.

Experts have learned a lot about the army from archaeological evidence. Fragments of metal Roman armor and weapons have been found on ancient battlefield sites such as Teutoburg Forest in Germany.

The *testudo* formation, "tortoise" in Latin, was a way for Roman legionaries to protect themselves.

The defeat at the Teutoburg Forest stunned the Romans.

In 9 CE, the Romans suffered a rare defeat when German warriors **ambushed** three legions in the forest. As they fled, the Romans dropped their weapons. The weapons were preserved in the woodland until an amateur archaeologist found them in 1987. Since then, archaeologists at the site have uncovered short swords used for stabbing, metal-tipped spears for throwing, and large rectangular shields.

↑ A ruined fort beside Hadrian's Wall in northern Britain.

The defeat at Teutoburg Forest sent shockwaves through the whole Roman Empire. It was Rome's first major defeat. The Emperor Augustus could not believe that his mighty army had suffered a defeat at the hands of German bandits.

Expanding the Empire

Each time the Roman army conquered a new territory, Roman engineers arrived. They built roads and ports, and Roman traders later arrived to buy and sell goods. The Roman conquerors then set about building towns and cities. They constructed buildings similar to those in Rome: a colosseum, theaters, baths, circuses for chariot races, a forum, and temples.

The Romans wanted to build versions of Rome across the empire to remind the conquered peoples that they were now part of the mighty Roman Empire. The emperors believed this was the best way to keep people loyal, even when they were far away from Rome itself. The strategy was reinforced by the army. Roman soldiers were left behind in the newly conquered lands. These soldiers were intended to protect the local people, but they were also there to defeat any uprisings against Roman rule by the local people.

A Northern Outpost

When Hadrian became emperor in 117 CE, there were 44 provinces in the Roman Empire. Hadrian visited 40 of them to make sure that the empire was being governed well.

ANCIENT SECRETS

Buried Coins

For archaeologists, digging up buried Roman coins is invaluable. The same coins, called *denarii*, were used throughout the empire. After 27 BCE, all coins carried a portrait of the current emperor at the time they were made. This makes Roman coins an easy way to date the layer of ground in which they are found.

Identifying the emperor on a Roman coin allows experts to date it precisely. →

25

↑ This Roman road still survives on a remote mountainside in Spain.

Hadrian ordered many structures to be built. One of the most famous is the wall named after him that still runs along the old border between England and Scotland.

Hadrian's Wall stretches 73 miles (117 km) between the east and west coasts across the narrowest part of northern Britain. Hadrian wanted the wall to protect his northernmost border from the Picts. The Picts were a warlike people who lived in what is now Scotland. The wall was manned by soldiers in small forts spaced a mile apart and in larger forts, which were spaced further apart. The Romans erected other walls and barriers to protect other parts of the empire from neighboring peoples. In what is now Germany, for example, the border was reinforced with a tall wooden fence.

Roman Roads

Rome also controlled its empire through its road network, which covered 50,000 miles (80,000 km). Stone roads were built as straight as possible across the landscape to cut journey times. The roads were used to move soldiers, to transport goods, and to carry messages. Soldiers built the roads, which were paid for by the government. Many roads were so well built they still survive.

Roman soldiers in Britain sent letters home. One man wrote asking for extra socks!

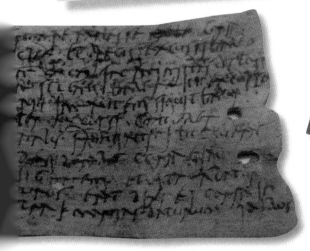

SCIENCE SOLVES IT

Lost Letters

In 1973, archaeologists found shavings of wood at a Roman fort on Hadrian's Wall. When they peeled two shavings apart, they revealed writing. Using **infrared** photography, the experts were able to see letters written on the wood by Roman soldiers. After more analysis, they could read the letters. The letters record how hard life was for a Roman soldier in northern England.

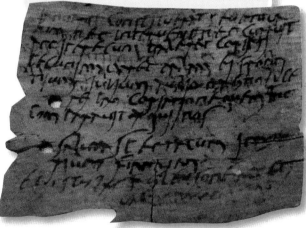

How Did the Romans Live?

Even though the ancient Romans lived around 2,000 years ago, archaeologists and other experts have found evidence to explain how people lived.

Ruined Roman buildings are one of the best sources of information. More clues come from the writings of Roman poets, playwrights, and historians who recorded daily life. Archaeologists are still discovering new information about how the Romans lived.

This Roman bathhouse was uncovered in Libya in North Africa.

Keeping Clean

Apart from the very poor, many ordinary Romans lived fairly comfortable lives. The emperors tried to keep their citizens happy by providing public facilities for them to use. One of the most popular pastimes was a bath. Roman bathhouses (*thermae*) were often built near natural springs so they had a constant supply of fresh water. If there were no springs, engineers built aqueducts to bring water to the baths.

During the reign of Emperor Augustus around 0–100 CE, Rome had 170 bathhouses. Three hundred years later, there were more than 900. Romans used the bathhouses as a meeting place, as well as a place to get clean. Some larger bathhouses had a games room, a restaurant, and even a library.

Modern Technology

Roman engineers created an early form of underfloor and central heating for use in bathhouses. Water was boiled in a furnace to create steam. The hot steam flowed through the hollow walls of the bathhouse and a gap beneath the floor called a hypocaust. The system was also used to heat the villas of wealthy Romans in colder parts of the empire, such as northern England.

In the bathhouse, bathers passed through a series of rooms. In the first room they took off their clothes. They entered the next room, which was called the *caldarium*. This was a steam room that made bathers sweat, which helped to clean their skin. Bathers rubbed their skin with perfumed oil, then used a small, curved metal tool called a *strigil* to scrape off the oil and dirt.

These pillars created space under the floor for hot air to circulate.

This wall painting shows a scene from a Roman kitchen.

When the heat grew too strong, the bather went to the next room. This *frigidarium* had a cold plunge pool to cool off in.

A Luxury Banquet

Romans also enjoyed eating. The writer Petronius lived in the first century CE. He described a feast at the home of a wealthy Roman. Diners lay on couches while slaves served them many courses. The food included fruit, olives, and honey. Baked dormice were a favorite **delicacy**. The Romans drank wine with their meals. They drank from lead goblets. At the time, no one knew that lead is a poison. The writer Apicius wrote a cookbook that gives details of recipes eaten by wealthy Roman families. Most Romans ate three meals a day.

The size of the Roman Empire meant there was lots choice for food. The fertile lands of North Africa and the Mediterranean supplied figs, grapes, olives, and grain. Romans made wine from the grapes and oil from the olives. They used the grain to make bread, which was the staple food. Trade routes brought spices, such as pepper and cinnamon, from Asia and Africa.

Food arrived by ship in Rome's port at Ostia, which was near the coast 15 miles (24 km) down the Tiber River from the city. It was carried to Rome in smaller boats. Rome's second port was Portus. In 2009, experts found a huge theater there.

Reading the Ruins

At the Forum in Rome, archaeologists have discovered inscriptions that identify some of the individual stores and workshops. Businesses included florists, perfumers, and jewelers.

In the cities, ordinary people lived in crowded apartment complexes. The rich lived in villas. Villas were often built outside cities and towns where there was more space.

SCIENCE SOLVES IT

Painted Villas

In 79 CE, a volcanic eruption destroyed the cities of Pompeii and Herculaneum. Rock called lava sealed the villas and preserved them for centuries. Scientists excavating the sites today have been able to see the exact colors the Romans painted their walls. They have even figured out exactly what materials the Romans used to make various paint colors.

This mural from a Roman villa shows various wild animals.

33

↑ This mosaic shows a large farmhouse on a Roman estate.

A typical Roman villa was built around a central courtyard. It had many rooms for the family. The walls were decorated with frescoes, and the floors had intricate mosaics set into them. Roman houses had little furniture compared with homes today. The furniture they did possess, however, would be familiar today—such as sofas, tables, and lamps.

Reading the Past

Experts study ancient texts to try to confirm what they learn from ruins and **artifacts**. In the 100s BCE, for example, the playwright Plautus described daily life in the Forum in Rome. He talks about the **moneylenders** and merchants there. Archaeologists have excavated some of the workshops and stores where these Roman businesspeople would have worked.

The Latin language of the Romans survived for thousands of years. It is still taught today and is the basis of languages such as Italian, Spanish, and French. This makes the written records of the Romans accessible for historians. However, the records usually tell stories from the point of view of the Romans—and not from the view of the peoples the Romans defeated and forced to join their empire.

ANCIENT SECRETS

Garum

One of the most popular of all foods in ancient Rome was garum. It was a sauce made by **fermenting** fish guts in salted water. Experts believe it probably resembled the fish sauce used today in Southeast Asian cooking. As the mixture brewed, it gave off a terrible smell. The stink was so bad that most Roman towns did not allow garum to be made. Instead, it was brewed in large stone vats outside towns.

Latin inscriptions in stone are easy to read—although parts of them may be missing.

Why Did Rome Fall?

One of the greatest mysteries about ancient Rome is why it collapsed. Over only a few centuries, Rome went from being the most powerful empire in the world to being overthrown.

The Roman Empire reached its greatest extent in 117 CE. Just 350 years later, Germanic invaders attacked Rome. They forced the last emperor in Rome, Romulus Augustus, to give up his throne. By then, the city's population had fallen to just 20,000. Much of the city lay abandoned. What had happened?

This painting shows the Emperor Honorius feeding birds. Rome's emperors lost power over time.

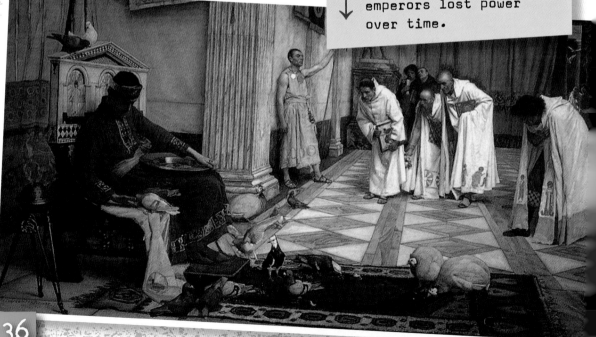

↑ Germanic warriors fight
Roman soldiers on the
edges of the Roman
Empire in Europe.

Under Threat

Modern experts believe that
there was not one single reason for the spectacular collapse
of the Roman Empire. Instead, they suggest that a number of
different pressures severely weakened the empire over centuries.

The most important factor was that the empire had grown too
large to be governed. The farthest provinces were thousands of
miles from Rome. It took weeks for messages to travel to or from
Rome or to move soldiers to defend the empire's borders against
invaders. The Romans called these invaders "barbarians," a word
that simply meant they were not Romans.

The defeat of the Roman army by Germanic warriors at Teutoburg Forest in 9 CE had shown that the Roman army was not unbeatable. From the 100s CE, barbarians started to attack Rome's borders more frequently. Some were Germanic peoples from the east, such as the Franks and Goths. They were being pushed westward by the Huns who lived to their east. In the west, the Vandals attacked Rome's empire in Spain and North Africa.

Weak Leadership

During this period, Rome also started to suffer from weak leadership. After years of strong rule by dictators and emperors, the government was now split by a struggle for power. The Senate and the army both wanted more say in running the empire. Emperors found themselves squeezed out of decision making. The Roman army killed emperors of which it disapproved. Over the next century, Rome had 37 emperors, of whom 25 were murdered by their enemies. This instability weakened the empire still further.

The Emperor Diocletian retired to live in a palace in Split, in what is now Croatia.

↑ The lead pipes beneath Rome may have poisoned the Romans who drank the water.

The Empire Splits

In 285, Emperor Diocletian decided the empire had grown too big to be governed from a single capital. To make day-to-day rule easier, Diocletian split the empire into two parts. The Western Roman Empire covered most of central and western Europe and western parts of North Africa. It had its capital at Rome.

SCIENCE SOLVES IT

Death by Poison

Historians had long been puzzled as to why wealthy Romans seemed to die at young ages, just like the poor, even though the poor had harder lives and worse food. It was only in the late 1900s that they figured out why. People have known for centuries that lead is poisonous. But experts hadn't realized just how much lead wealthy Romans came into contact with. Romans used lead goblets and utensils, and water was piped into their homes through lead pipes. They even added lead to their wine to sweeten the taste.

The Eastern Empire included the Balkans, Greece, Turkey, Egypt, and the Middle East. Its capital was at Constantinople (present-day Istanbul in Turkey). Diocletian became emperor in the east. He made Maximian, an army officer, the ruler of the Western Empire. Later, two emperors ruled each part of the empire together.

Diocletian's division of the empire failed. While the Eastern Empire remained prosperous, the decline of the Western Empire continued. The emperors failed to recover their power. The army was no longer strong enough to control barbarian raids and uprisings against Roman rule. It became more difficult to find good soldiers in the provinces. Many new recruits were not properly trained before going into action. The army lost many battles it would have won in the past.

A Roman moneylender counts coins. By the 400s, Rome's finances were in crisis.

No More Money

As well as its political and military weakness, Rome also suffered a financial crisis. The Roman Empire in the West was no longer wealthy. Emperors such as Commodus, who reigned in the 180s CE, had wasted huge amounts of money on personal luxuries, from huge palaces to vast banquets. By the 300s, paying for the army to defend the empire's borders and control the provinces cost so much that there was little money left to spend on **infrastructure**.

Rome's famous wealth had been wasted by its rulers.

The government could no longer afford to pay for maintenance. Roads and bridges fell into disrepair. The great public buildings around the Forum in Rome could no longer be maintained.

Economic Weakness

The Roman Empire had grown rich on agriculture. It controlled fertile farmland in North Africa and western Europe. By the 300s and 400s, however, agriculture had become big business. Individual farms had grown so large that they could only be profitable if they used slaves to provide free labor.

The last Roman emperor, Romulus Augustus, surrenders to the Visigoth Theodoric.

Rome's empire in the East adopted the Orthodox form of Christianity. ↑

Smaller farmers could not compete. They gave up and quit, causing high levels of unemployment. The few large farms that remained did not produce enough grain to feed all the Romans. The emperor had to import grain to make bread for the citizens. This cost more money.

With fewer people working and with more provinces rebelling, Rome was no longer able to collect enough taxes from the empire. The treasury had so little gold that the emperors ordered the amount of gold used in Roman coins to be reduced. Traders panicked and raised their prices. This led to a general rise in prices, a process known as inflation. Although ordinary Romans could no longer afford to buy bread, the emperors continued to spend freely on their luxurious lifestyles.

The Empire Ends

By the mid-400s, repeated raids by barbarians on the edges of the Roman Empire had greatly weakened it. Germanic warriors known as Visigoths struck the fatal blow. In 476, the Visigoths **sacked** Rome. The Visigothic ruler, Theodoric, threw Emperor Romulus Augustus off the throne and became ruler in his place.

The Roman amphitheater in Palmyra in Syria was damaged by terrorists in the 2010s.

IN CONTEXT

Preserving Roman Ruins
Experts face a challenge to protect Roman ruins. One problem is that there are simply so many. They stand throughout Europe, North Africa, and the Middle East. In Europe, construction threatens many sites. In the Middle East and Africa, the threat comes from warfare. Experts try to preserve key sites and record the contents of other sites that might be lost.

The Colosseum in Rome is one of the world's most popular tourist sites. ↑

The Western Roman Empire had ended. Across Europe, trade slowed down and people abandoned Roman cities. Latin, which had been spoken everywhere, was now only spoken by a few priests and others.

The Eastern Empire

In the east, the Roman Empire became known as Byzantium. It survived until 1453, when its capital city, Constantinople, was conquered by the Ottoman Turks. Some historians see 1453 as the end of the Roman Empire. For most experts, however, the real Roman Empire was the one with its capital in the city of Rome— and that had ended nearly 1,000 years earlier.

Glossary

ambushed Launched a surprise attack.

amphitheater An open building for public events, with banks of seats arranged in tiers.

aqueduct An artificial channel to carry water.

archaeologists People who study the past by examining old ruins, objects, and records.

artifacts Objects made by human beings, usually with a cultural or historical value.

assassinated Murdered for a political reason.

ceremonial Used for formal political or religious occasions.

concrete A building material made from gravel, sand, cement, and water.

delicacy A favorite and unusual food.

dictators Rulers who have complete control over a country.

empire A large group of countries ruled by the same emperor or empress.

excavating Methodically uncovering and recording objects buried beneath the ground.

fermenting Changing as a result of the actions of organisms such as bacteria or yeast.

gladiators Men trained to fight against other men or animals in an arena.

infrared Describes a type of light that is not visible to the human eye.

infrastructure The structures needed to run a country, such as roads and sewerage.

moneylenders People who loan money in return for a fee called interest.

mosaics Pictures made of small pieces of colored stone, glass, or pottery.

occupation The state of being occupied by a military force.

peninsula A piece of land surrounded by water on three sides.

radiocarbon dating A way of find out the age of an object by measuring how much carbon it contains.

republic A state in which people choose representatives to run the government.

sacked Plundered and destroyed.

strategy A long-term plan for achieving a particular goal.

terracotta A type of red clay pottery.

.

Further Resources

Books

Anderson, Zachary. *The Fall of Rome and the Rise of Constantinople*. Exploring the Ancient and Medieval Worlds. New York: Cavendish Square Publishing, 2015.

Dubois, Muriel L. *Ancient Rome: A Mighty Empire*. Great Civilizations. Mankato, Minn: Capstone Press, 2012.

Hinds, Kathryn. *The City*. Life in the Roman Empire. New York: Cavendish Square Publishing, 2004.

James, Simon. *Ancient Rome*. DK Eyewitness Books. New York: DK Children's, 2015.

Kerrigan, Michael. *Romans*. Ancients in their Own Words. New York: Cavendish Square Publishing, 2010.

Websites

www.bbc.co.uk/education/topics/zwmpfg8
BBC Bitesize features learners' guides about Rome as well as helpful video clips.

www.dkfindout.com/uk/history/ancient-rome/
This page about the city of Rome features an interactive cutaway diagram of the Colosseum.

www.ducksters.com/history/ancient_rome.php
This page has fun facts, a map of ancient Rome, and links to many other subjects about the Romans.

www.historyforkids.net/ancient-rome.html
This website provides a directory of all sorts of different pages about Rome, from its origins to government and daily life.

www.ngkids.co.uk/history/10-facts-about-the-ancient-Romans
This National Geographic Kids website features ten fascinating facts about the ancient Romans.

Publisher's note to educators and parents: Our editors have carefully reviewed these websites to ensure that they are suitable for students. Many websites change frequently, however, and we cannot guarantee that a site's future contents will continue to meet our high standards of quality and educational value. Be advised that students should be closely supervised whenever they access the Internet.

Index